Superstars
of the
NEW ENGLAND
PATRIOTS

by Matt Scheff

LIBRARY

amicus
high interest

Amicus High Interest is published by Amicus
P.O. Box 1329, Mankato, MN 56002
www.amicuspublishing.us

Library of Congress Cataloging-in-Publication Data
Scheff, Matt.
  Superstars of the New England Patriots / Matt Scheff.
    pages cm. -- (Pro sports superstars)
  Includes index.
  ISBN 978-1-60753-527-0 (hardcover) -- ISBN 978-1-60753-557-7 (eBook)
  1. New England Patriots (Football team)--History--Juvenile literature. I.
Title.
  GV956.N36S36 2014
  796.332'640974461--dc23
                          2013010398

Photo Credits: Winslow Townson/AP Images, cover; Pro Football Hall
of Fame/AP Images, 2, 9; David Drapkin/AP Images, 5; NFL Photos/AP
Images, 6, 13, 14; Mike Kullen/AP Images, 10; Stephan Savoia/AP Images,
17; G. Newman Lowrance/AP Images, 18; Tom DiPace/AP Images, 21, 22

Produced for Amicus by The Peterson Publishing Company
and Red Line Editorial.

Editor Jenna Gleisner
Designer Becky Daum
Printed in the United States of America
Mankato, MN
12-2013
PO1187
10 9 8 7 6 5 4 3 2

TABLE OF CONTENTS

MEET THE NEW ENGLAND PATRIOTS

The New England Patriots have played in seven Super Bowls. They won three of them. The Patriots have had many great players. Here are some of the best.

JOHN HANNAH

John Hannah was a strong blocker. His **rookie** year was 1973. He was quick. The other team could not get by him. He made nine **Pro Bowls**. He helped the Patriots get to a Super Bowl.

MIKE HAYNES

Mike Haynes was a star on **defense**. He was the **NFL** Defensive Rookie of the Year in 1976. He was fast. He **intercepted** many passes. Haynes played seven seasons with the Patriots.

Morgan led the NFL with 12 touchdown catches in 1979.

STANLEY MORGAN

Stanley Morgan loved to catch long passes. He was very fast. He was good at getting open. Morgan played 13 seasons for the Patriots.

ANDRE TIPPETT

Andre Tippett was a great **tackler**. He was fast. He hit hard. Tippett got a lot of **sacks**. He was picked to play five Pro Bowls in a row. The first was in 1984.

Tippett has made more sacks than any other Patriots player.

BRUCE ARMSTRONG

Bruce Armstrong started 212 games. That is the most of any Patriot. Armstrong was strong and quick. He was also smart. He went to six Pro Bowls. He retired in 2001.

DREW BLEDSOE

Drew Bledsoe was a good passer. He had a very strong arm. Bledsoe led the 1996 Patriots to the Super Bowl.

The Patriots picked Bledsoe first overall in the 1993 draft.

TEDY BRUSCHI

Tedy Bruschi wasn't big. But he was smart and tough. He helped the Patriots win three Super Bowls. The last one was in 2005. He played 13 seasons for the Patriots.

TOM BRADY

Tom Brady may be the best **quarterback** ever. He has led the Patriots to five Super Bowls. He has won two **MVP** awards.

The Patriots have had many great stars. Some have made the Hall of Fame. Who will be the next star?

Brady threw 50 touchdown passes in 2007. That is still an NFL record.

TEAM FAST FACTS

Founded: 1960

Other Names: Boston Patriots (1960-1970)

Nickname: The Pats

Home Stadium: Gillette Stadium (Foxboro, Massachusetts)

Super Bowl Titles: 3 (2001, 2003, and 2004)

Hall of Fame Players: 4, including John Hannah, Mike Haynes, and Andre Tippett

WORDS TO KNOW

defense – the group of players that tries to stop the other team from scoring

intercept – when the opponent catches a pass

MVP – Most Valuable Player; an honor given to the best player each season

NFL – National Football League; the league pro football players play in

Pro Bowl – the NFL's all-star game

quarterback – a player whose main jobs are to lead the offense and throw passes

rookie – a player in his first season

sack – a tackle of the quarterback on a passing play

tackler – a player whose main job is knocking players on the other team to the ground so they cannot score

LEARN MORE

Books

Frisch, Aaron. *New England Patriots*. Mankato, MN: Creative Education, 2011.

MacRae, Sloan. *The New England Patriots*. New York: PowerKids Press, 2011.

Web Sites

New England Patriots—Official Site
http://www.patriots.com
Watch video clips and view photos of the New England Patriots.

NFL.com
http://nfl.com
Check out pictures and your favorite football players' stats.

NFL Rush
http://www.nflrush.com
Play games and learn how to be a part of NFL PLAY 60.

INDEX